MOST FAMOUS
& INFLUENTIAL
PEOPLE IN THE
WOLRD

Contents

The most famous and influential people in the world today:

Few people spend their entire lives earning fame, but as you know, fame is an invisible and difficult concept to quantify. Most of us draw inspiration from people from all walks of life: celebrities, politicians, business people, and great living legends in our industry.

So what makes someone famous? What qualifies for being on the list of the most influential people in history? The most intelligent people of all time deserve the top rankings. Each of these remarkable and inspiring people used the power of their intellect to change the world.

Maybe they changed our perception of the world and ourselves. You can call them gods, leaders, influencers, great thinkers, fathers, philosophers, or anything else. This article describes the ten most famous figures in world history. This list includes scientists, religious people, and investors. The collection also includes some of the most influential figures in world history.

1. Jesus Christ:

Jesus Christ was born in Bethlehem, Palestine. He was born of Mary, who, according to the Bible, gave birth to a child of the Holy Spirit (Matthew 1:18). He was both human and divine(John 20:28). According to the Bible, He is the only God (Deuteronomy 6:4).

According to Christian scriptures, Jesus' mission on earth was to bring salvation and salvation to the world. He healed the sick, raised the dead, forgave our sins, died on the cross for this world, and prepared for us the way to salvation while on earth. He begged the Almighty to forgive those who wanted him to die on the cross. On the third day, he rose again. Jesus died on the cross to redeem us from our sins. Both the unleavened bread and the grape harvest were spiritually present during the Eucharist. He was probably the most famous person to ever walk this planet. Perhaps not everyone is adept at all aspects of life. On the other hand, the name of Jesus Christ is known. Jesus is the head of Christianity and people see him as the most important person on earth because of their faith in him.

2. Mohammed:

Muhammad (AD 570 – 632) was an Arab prophet best known as a major figure (and the last prophet) of Islam and one of the world's most respected and important historical figures. considered to be one. Muhammad is considered by non-Muslims to be the founder of Islam. He found nothing among the Muslims because the religion known as Islam already existed and needed to be revived to its proper state. Muslims believe that Muhammad revived the religion, putting it together under the ideas that God revealed to him in his recorded revelations. From there the Qur'an was born. Islam is an Arabic word meaning "surrender" or "surrender", in this case, the Will of Allah. Mohammed. Like Nuh, Musa, Saleh, Moses, and Jesus Christ, Muhammad was God's last messenger and prophet. Muhammad revived Islam and brought it to non-Muslims. He was the only one to record the words of God that would later become the Quran.

3. Adolf Hitler:

Adolf Hitler (April 20, 1889 – April 30, 1945) was a German politician who led the Nazi party and ruled as chancellor and leader of Germany. He was a key figure in the Holocaust there and the Nazis, as his German leader, attacked Poland in 1939 to start World War II. As you know, that is the root cause of World War II. He tailored it to satisfy two deep desires.

To be the most powerful person on the planet, preferably in history if not the whole world. And, for his pleasure, he inflicted as much pain as possible on all those whom he blamed for Germany's humiliating and disastrous defeat in the First World War and for the extreme poverty during the war. rice field. The most influential people of the 21st century

After World War I, Germany was forced to pay the war costs of all other countries, and the German economy was completely destroyed. Deutsche marks have been devalued to such an extent that young people burn millions of marks at once to keep warm on the streets.

He was a very good man of the twentieth century. Today's textbooks are full of Hitler myths. He is one of the most despised people on earth. He is also responsible for the murder of approximately 5.8 million people, including Jews, children, artisans, women, and others. During World War II, he committed suicide before Germany was defeated.

4. Albert Einstein:

Albert He Einstein was born on March 14, 1879, in Ulm, Württemberg, Germany. He died on April 18, 1955. He began his education at the Luitpold Gymnasium in Germany. Albert resumed his studies in 1896 in Zurich, Switzerland, where he studied physics and mathematics.

One of the two foundations of modern physics is the theoretical physicist Albert Einstein. He won the Nobel Prize in Physics for his theory of photoelectric phenomena. After being persecuted by the Nazi Party in Germany, he emigrated to the United States the next decade. His discoveries inspired the emergence of atomic energy. In his later years, Einstein focused on unified theory. Albert Einstein is often considered the most prominent physicist of the twentieth century because of his insatiable curiosity.

5. Abraham Lincoln:

Lincoln led the most powerful nation in the world through the bloodiest war, the American Civil War. Not only was Lincoln president famous for preserving the Union during the Civil War, but his Gettysburg Address also inspired millions around the world. He was President of the United States until his assassination.

Lincoln professed during his presidential campaign that he was against slavery. Many Southerners believed that if elected, he would actually try to abolish slavery in the United States and cause disaster. Or a coalition was formed. Four other people then joined the group. The war took its toll, but Lincoln promised to unite the Union army.

Fighting broke out in April 1861. Lincoln always called the Civil War a battle to save the Union Army, but in January 1863 he issued the Provisional Emancipation Proclamation, freeing all slaves in Confederate-controlled areas. This was an important symbolic move that defined the Union campaign as a fight to abolish slavery. By declaring martial law and suspending the judiciary, Lincoln used more power than any president before him to win the war. Until Ulysses S. Grant became commander-in-chief in 1864, he had trouble recruiting strong generals to lead the Union army. He was assassinated in 1865.

6. Leonardo da Vinci:

Leonardo da Vinci was born on April 15, 1452, in the town of Vinci, the illegitimate son of a local lawyer. In Florence, he apprenticed to both the sculptor and painter Andrea del Verrocchio, and by 1478 he had established himself as an independent master. Da Vinci was one of the most prominent artists and sculptors of the Italian Renaissance, as well as an exceptional engineer, scientist, and inventor. He died on his 2nd May 1519. Although the success of his historic paintings made da Vinci primarily known as an artist, the hundreds of pages of his writings reveal the most diverse and brightest thoughts. He wrote and used a wide range of subjects, including geography, anatomy (which he learned to better represent the human body), flight, gravity, and optics. He was 600 years ahead of his time when he "invented" the bicycle, the airplane, and the parachute.

If all of this research had been presented in an understandable way, da Vinci's status as a revolutionary scientist would have been undeniable. His real talent, however, was not only as a scientist and an artist but as a combined "artist and engineer". His art is scientific and grounded in extensive research into the mechanics of the human body and the physics of light and shadow. His science is presented through art, and his paintings and drawings show what he said and how he saw how the universe worked.

7. William Shakespeare:

The man who has received the most votes in the history of mankind as an outstanding writer in English or any other language is arguably the source of some of the words and phrases widely used in his native language today. . The King

James Bible accounts for about half of the common English idioms, with the rest coming from his Bard's dictionary. The most surprising aspect of Shakespeare's reputation is how little is known about Shakespeare, the man, and his life. Before he became a playwright, he worked as an actor only in high school. It is the perfect blend of Shakespeare's finest poetry, profound multidimensional philosophy, and lively wit that sets him apart.

Once done, he won many awards and is considered a great writer. Shakespeare did it 37 times, not including 154 sonnets that form the core of the English repertoire. Hamlet and King Lear is a universally recognized masterpiece that sets a milestone for all other dramas before and after it.

8. Isaac Newton:

The discoverer of calculus, Albert demoted Einstein to 10th place. Einstein would have jumped to the top of Google searches alone (6.1 million per month), but there are many more books about Newton. Einstein is on track to break Newton's record that he is well below 286 years, but if so, Einstein's theory of relativity would have had no basis if Newton hadn't lived. Isaac Newton alone is responsible for 95% of all classical mechanics. He extended the binomial theorem, built the reflecting telescope, introduced the concept of "gravity", and delivered the final blow to the geocentric dominance of the Roman Catholic Church. The Inquisition was held against Copernicus and Galileo, but no one challenged Newton's Principia Mathematica.

It is foolish to refute the observations of others, but in Newton's situation, it was impossible to refute mathematics. He disproved his first two heliocentric theories, revealing how and why all macroscopic objects in the universe move the way they do. Even though he did everything himself and was busy with sex, he always had time to explore visual elements and principles and develop Petdoor. Died at the age of 84, still a virgin.

9. Siddhartha Gautama (France):

Gautama was most likely born in 563 BC. She was Kapilavastu or Lumbini in Nepal and Babylon sacked Jerusalem when she was about 24 years old. Gautama was a mortal man who experienced nirvana, or spiritual awakening and peace of mind, at the age of 35 while sitting under the Pipal tree, now known as the Bodhi tree, in Bodh Gaya, India.

The present tree, which grew from the seed of the original tree, was planted in 288 BC. sowing. Buddha meditated for seven weeks until he understood how to eliminate the suffering of every individual on earth. People must follow his teachings in order to get rid of various diseases in life.

Gautama, the supreme Buddha, is also worshiped
in Hinduism as one of his ten manifestations of
Vishnu, the supreme deity. Gautama is also

worshiped by the Baha'i as a mortal manifestation of God who came to teach mankind how to love one another and live in peace and contentment. Gautama is said to have lived in 411 BC. He must be over 150 years old and dead. So. According to modern researchers, his death was around 483, at the age of 80.

10. Barack Obama:

Barack Obama, the first African-American elected president of the United States, has a net worth of at least $70 million, according to International Business Times. According to The New York Post, the net worth of the 44th former president of the United States exceeds $130 million as of 2021.

Obama resigned from the presidency in 2005 until he served as a senator from Illinois until 2008. He ran for president in 2007 and 2008 and won the party's nomination. That same year, he was elected president, defeating Republican presidential nominee John McCain. His fame skyrocketed after he was named a Nobel Peace Prize laureate in 2009.

But even after White left the House, Obama remained a powerful figure. His latest memoir, Promised Land, was released in 2020 and sold millions of copies in just days of its release. His posts and videos are shared widely on his social media sites such as Facebook and Twitter. It is believed that he earned $400,000 a year during his presidency and received a $200,000 annual pension as a former president. From speaking at public events to signing a production deal with Netflix, Obama is believed to have had a reasonably successful life after completing his term as President of the United States. Obama ranks tenth on the list of the world's most famous people.

11. Donald Trump:

Donald Trump tops the list of the most famous people in the world. The former President of the United States has been the focus of much debate over the years due to his flamboyant and ambiguous personality. rice field. Additionally, you may recognize his name as the host of the television apprentice and beauty pageant Miss He is the owner of the Universe series.

Forbes put Donald Trump's net worth at $2.1 billion in the 2020 Billionaires Rankings. Trump gained national attention not only as a tough businessman but also as a writer. Trump's book, The Art of the Deal, was hailed as a New York Times bestseller. Without a doubt, Donald his Trump is now one of the most famous people in the world.

12. Michael Jackson:

Michael Jackson is next on our list. Known as the "King of Pop," Michael Jackson is one of the most prominent and influential figures in 20th-century culture. Michael Jackson is now considered by many to be an idol and a role model for famous and aspiring artists. He holds 16 Guinness World Records and is one of the greatest musicians of all time. There is also.

This is also a highly unusual honor unique to him, being the first and only recorded artist to be inducted into both the National Dance Museum and the Hall of Fame. In addition to numerous world records, Michael Jackson invented famous dance moves such as the moonwalk and robots and continues to inspire young dancers around the world. An accomplished musician and charismatic performer, Michael Jackson revolutionized the art

of music through his videos and helped establish modern pop music. His tremendous influence extends beyond the world of music.

13. Justin Bieber:

Famous pop musician Justin Bieber needs no introduction. A boy who began sharing videos of himself singing on his YouTube with his relatives and friends launched his pop-star career. It wasn't until his videos gained viral likes and subscribers that he gained more than his 10,000,000 subscribers.

His movies are very popular on his Facebook. His road to fame continued when he began contract negotiations with R&B superstar Usher. His debut album, My World, sold over one million copies in the United States alone. Hailed as the "Prince of Pop," he overtook Lady Gaga to become Twitter's most-followed user in 2013.

Additionally, he won a Grammy Award in 2016 and now has over 50 million subscribers on his YouTube channel. He was also the first male solo

artist to top both the Top 100 and 200 of the Billboard charts consecutively with his song "Peaches", which was his first to top the Billboard charts. was his project's eighth number one. Over the years, his fame has allowed him to undertake several successful commercial ventures.

Most Popular People in The World Currently

1. Elon Musk:

Elon Musk is the CEO of Tesla Inc and SpaceX. He is the richest person in the world as of 2022 he has a net worth of $239.6 billion. Elon Musk owns multiple companies including Zip2, X.com, PayPal, SpaceX, The Musk Foundation, Tesla, SolarCity, and OpenAI.

He is best known for Tesla, SpaceX, Neuralink, The Boring Company, and most recently Twitter. He owns a 23% stake in Tesla, the electric car company he co-founded in 2003. He is changing movements on earth and between earth and space.

Elon Musk is number one on our list, but not only has his recent acquisition of Twitter gone viral, but we're skeptical that he plans to make more acquisitions. US-based news magazine Time named Elon Musk his 2021 Person of the Year on Dec. 13 on Time's Magane.

2. Dwayne Johnson:

Dwayne Johnson is widely known for his WWE alias The Rock. He is one of the most popular figures in the world, known for his roles as a professional wrestler, actor, and businessman. He wrestled for eight years before retiring from his WWE Championship to pursue an acting career.

The Rock has a net worth of around $320 million making him one of the highest-paid actors. He is also one of the most followed actors as his social media life is widely followed.

3. Cristiano Ronaldo:

Christiano Ronaldo is considered one of the best soccer players in the world and has the most followers on Facebook.

He has had great records with Manchester United, Real Madrid, Juventus, and the Portuguese national team. Cristiano Ronaldo currently play for Al-Nassr in Saudi Arabia. He has won the World Player of the Year award five times, a feat that rivals Lionel Messi and was his equal at first. His assets are:

For $500 million, he's signed up for Nike boots.

4. Lionel Messi:

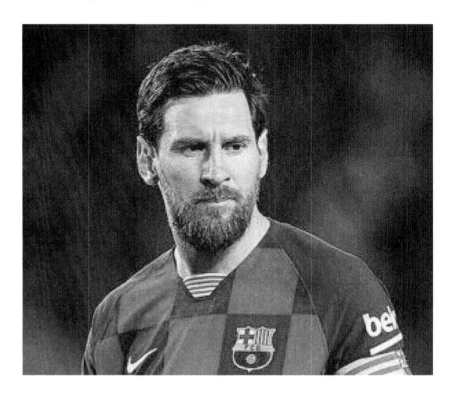

Lionel Andres Messi, popularly known as Leo Messi. He is an Argentinian professional footballer who plays the forward position for Argentina and is the captain of the Argentine national team. He is considered by many sports commentators to be the best footballer in the world.

Lionel Messi has won many awards including the Baron d'Or seven times and has been the top scorer for his country and club many times. In fact, Messi is one of the most famous people in the world due to the many influences his career has had on him. Currently play for Paris Saint German in France.

5. Joe Biden:

Joseph Robinette Biden Jr. is an American politician and the 46th President of the United States. He also served as Vice President under President Barack Obama from 2009 until 2017.

Joe Biden is the most glasses-wearing person in 2021, the year he took office as the 46th President of the United States, with many celebrities and politicians endorsing him, and his support for Trump. The victory has become one of the most popular of all presidential elections. time.

6. Mark Zuckerberg:

Mark Zuckerberg is just a self-made millionaire he became a millionaire at the age of 23. He is the founder of his one of the world's most popular apps called Facebook, now called Meta.

Mark Zuckerberg was raised as a Reform Jew and was later identified as an atheist. In 2016 he issued the following statement:

"I grew up Jewish and had a period of time when I questioned many things, but now I believe that religion is very important."

According to the Bloomberg Billionaires Index, a ranking of the world's richest people, Mark Zuckerberg is the 10th richest person in the world with a net worth of $89.6 billion. He earned $11 billion in a single day, making him the 18th to 10th richest person in the world.

7. Jeff Bezos:

Jeff Bezos is an American entrepreneur, media owner, investor, computer engineer, and commercial astronaut. He is the founder of Amazon. Despite being a wealthy person worth over $100 billion, Bezos wasn't born into a wealthy family. His parents were 18 and he was

17 when he was born. Today, Jeff Bezos is one of the richest and most popular people in the world and has backed many writers and producers with his company. This is proof that your background does not determine your future.

6. Vladimir Putin

Vladimir Putin is a former intelligence officer who has been president of Russia since 2012, and before that he was president from 1999 until he was in 2008. He worked as a foreign intelligence officer for the KGB for 16 years until he resigned in 1991 to pursue his political career in St. Petersburg.

Under his first term as president, the country's economy grew for eight consecutive years. This growth was the result of a five-fold increase in the price of oil and gas, which makes up the majority of Russia's exports, a recovery from the post-communist recession and financial crisis, a surge in foreign investment, and a cautious economy and fiscal policy. was brought as policy. Background

Born in Leningrad (now St. Petersburg), Putin's mother was a factory worker and his father was a Soviet Navy conscript in his early 1930s. He began practicing sambo and judo at the age of 12 and enjoyed reading about Marx, Engels, and

Lenin. He learned German at that age and speaks it as a second language.

He graduated from St. Petersburg State University with a law faculty in 1975 and entered the KGB. In 1984, Putin was sent to Moscow for further training at the Yuri Andropov Red Banner Institute and worked in Dresden, East Germany as a translator, using the cover identity. According to Putin's official biography, in 1989 he kept files from the Soviet Cultural Center in Dresden and a KGB villa for the official authorities of a unified Germany, and protesters, including KGB and Stasi agents, obtained them. prevented it from being destroyed. He explained that many documents were left in Germany only for the blast furnace, but many documents from the KGB mansion were sent to Moscow.

Putin resigned from the KGB in 1991 after the coup against Mikhail Gorbachev.

Entering Politics

In June 1991, he became Chairman of the Mayor's Office's Foreign Relations Committee, responsible for international relations and the promotion of foreign investment. Less than a year later, he was investigated by the city's legislative council. allowed to do Despite recommendations to remove Putin, he remained chief until 1996.

In 1994 he was appointed first vice-president of the St. Petersburg government, and in May 1995, he organized the St. Petersburg branch of Our Home – Russia, a pro-government political party, which remained in the branch until June 1997. served as chairman of

In 1997, President Boris Yeltsin appointed Putin as Deputy Chief of the General Staff, a position he held until May 1998. Yeltsin then appointed him head of the Federal Security Service, the main intelligence agency of the Russian Federation and successor to the KGB.

In August 1999, Putin was appointed one of his three first deputy prime ministers and agreed to run for president at Yeltsin's request the same day.

Presidential Term

On December 31, 1999, Yeltsin abruptly resigned and Putin became Acting President of the Russian

Federation, in accordance with the Russian Constitution. From 2000 to 2004, Putin won a power struggle against Russian oligarchs and set out to rebuild the impoverished country.

During the 2002 Moscow theater hostage crisis, much of the international media warned that the deaths of 130 of his hostages in a special forces rescue operation would undermine Putin's popularity. garnered him a record 83 approval rating.

Printed in Great Britain
by Amazon

37188110R00036